Let's Sing and Learn in FRENCH

MATT MAXWELL

CD EDITION

McGraw·Hill

New York   Chicago   San Francisco   Lisbon   London   Madrid   Mexico City
Milan   New Delhi   San Juan   Seoul   Singapore   Sydney   Toronto

Preface

Let's Sing and Learn in French is a delightful collection of 12 songs—some original, some traditional—arranged with a distinctly modern flair. They are all designed to teach children basic French vocabulary and expressions in a fresh, exciting way. The songs are easy *and* fun to sing, making them the ideal medium for introducing children to the words, accent, and rhythms of the French language.

Through this collection, young people will learn basic greetings in French, parts of the body, names of animals, means of transportation, and more. The musical scores contained in this book allow any teacher or parent with a minimal knowledge of, say, the guitar or keyboards to accompany children as they sing.

The CD that accompanies this songbook features all 12 songs, performed by Matt Maxwell, his musicians, and a group of children. Ranging in style from folk to rock 'n' roll, these engaging renditions have been expertly recorded and are sure to inspire young people to their best singing efforts. The CD will also provide children with an excellent model for French pronunciation and intonation.

The joyful melodies in *Let's Sing and Learn in French* assure that a child's first introduction to French will be both pleasurable and motivating.

7 8 9 0   MAL/MAL   2 1

ISBN 0-07-143178-0 (book)
ISBN 0-07-142143-2 (book and CD package)

McGraw-Hill books are available at special quantity discounts to use as premiums and sales promotions, or for use in corporate training programs. For more information, please write to the Director of Special Sales, Professional Publishing, McGraw-Hill, Two Penn Plaza, New York, NY 10121-2298. Or contact your local bookstore.

This book is printed on acid-free paper.

Table des Matières
Table of Contents

4

Voici les accords pour la guitare.
Here are the guitar chords.

A
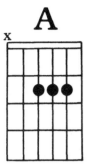

B
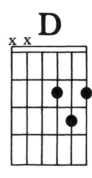

C
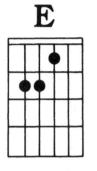

D
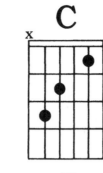

E
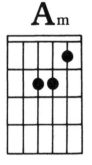

F
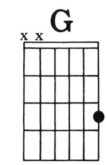

G
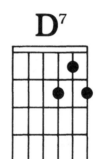

E$_m$
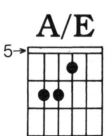

A$_m$
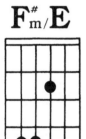

A^7
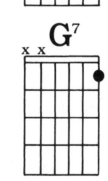

A/E
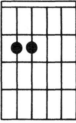

D^7
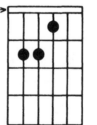

C^7
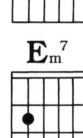

F$^{\#}_m$/E
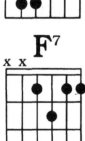

G$^{\#}_m$/E
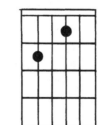

G^7
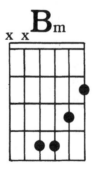

B/E
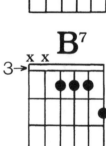

E$_m$^{7}

F^7

F$^{\#}_m$

E^7

B$_m$

B^7

Rock & Roll Frère Jacques

Cette chanson figure parmi les plus populaires auprès des enfants, paraît-il. Je trouve assez amusante l'ideé du vieux Frère Jacques, qui après tant de siècles, se met finalement au rock & roll. Rien de tel que de "jiver" au son de cette chanson du bon vieux temps!

From all accounts this seems to be most kids' favorite song. I guess the notion of old Frère Jacques, after all these centuries, finally learning to rock is kind of funny. This is a great song to do some good old-fashioned jiving to!

Rock & Roll Frère Jacques

Paroles & musique par/
Words & music by: Matt

8

Frère Jacques, frère Jacques, dansez-vous?
Frère Jacques, frère Jacques, dansez-vous?
On joue, on joue du Rock & Roll!
Ding dang dong dong
Ding dang dong . . .

C'est l'Halloween

L'Halloween est une fête très différente des autres. C'est l'occasion de se déguiser et de devenir la créature de ses rêves ou…de ses cauchemars. Pour créer une ambiance, essayez de trouver des instruments à percussion qui donnent la chair de poule. Par exemple, battez une cymbale (mais doucement!) avec une grande cuillère en bois. Ça fait frémir!

Halloween is such a great time of year. For this one day you can become the person or creature of your wildest dreams (or nightmares…). When you play this song, see if you can find or make percussion instruments that make creepy sounds. For instance, hit a cymbal (softly!) with a big wooden spoon. It'll make you shiver!

C'est l'Halloween

Paroles & musique par/
Words & music by: Matt

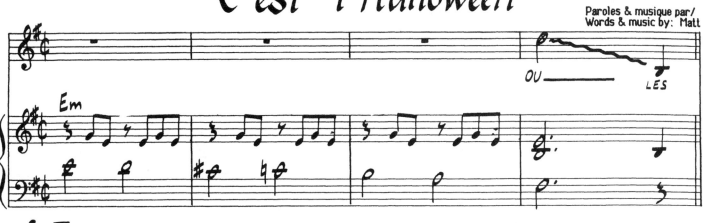

OU _____ LES

SOR- CIÈRES SORTENT LE SOIR LES FAN- TÔMES AUS-

SI LE CIEL EST TOUT NOIR

LES NU- AGES SONT GRIS EST-CE QUE TU AS

PEUR DES MÉ - CHANTS ES - PRITS ?

Ô MON - SIEUR, OUI, OUI, OUI, OUI,

OUI ! _____ C'EST l'HALL- O - WEEN—

_____ C'EST _____ l'HALL- O - WEEN, HÉ !

Pendant l'Halloween
Tu peux être ce que tu veux
Un tigre féroce
Ou un serpent bleu
Il se fait tard, rentres-tu à la maison?
Ô Madame, non, non, non!

Refrain

La lune, elle est pleine
Le hibou, il crie
De toutes les branches
Pendent des chauves-souris
Est-ce que tu as peur de cette nuit?
Ô Madame, oui, oui, oui!

Refrain

Le chat angora

Voici une histoire amusante où la souris bat le chat à son propre jeu. Des "kazoos" et des harmonicas feraient un bon accompagnement.

This is a funny story about a mouse who beats a cat at his own game. This is a good one to play with kazoos and harmonicas.

Le chat angora

Traditionnelle – nouvelles paroles par/
Traditional – new verses by: Matt

(RI.) IL É-TAIT UNE FOIS ET-CE-TE-RA, ET- CE - TE- RA. UN CHAT AN - GO.___

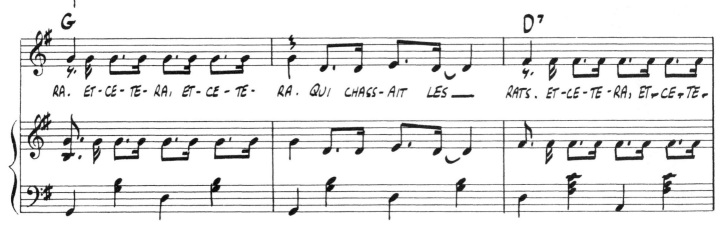

RA. ET-CE-TE-RA, ET-CE-TE- RA. QUI CHASS-AIT LES___ RATS. ET-CE-TE-RA, ET-CE-TE-

RA. DANS LE SA-HA___ RA. ET-CE-TE-RA, ET-CE-TE- RA. IL A-VAIT SUR___

fine

Il avait surpris	"Je sais que tu as faim	"Hélas, qu'est-ce que j'ai fait?
Etceteri, etceteri	Etceterin, etceterin	Etceteré, etceteré
Dans un sac de riz	Mais si tu veux manger, eh bien	Il s'est en allé
Etceteri, etceteri	Etceterin, etceterin	Etceteré, etceteré
Un petit rat tout gris	Il te faut du pain	Maintenant je n'ai
Etceteri, etceteri	Etceterin, etceterin	Etceteré, etceteré
Gros comme une souris	Et un peu de vin"	Que mon pain à manger!"
Etceteri, etceteri	Etceterin, etceterin	Etceteré, etceteré
"Je vais te manger"	Le chat est donc parti	*Répétez la première strophe*
Etceteré, etceteré	Etceteri, etceteri	
"Mais oui, je le sais,"	Pour l'épicerie	
Etceteré, etceteré	Etceteri, etceteri	
Mais avant de diner	Il est rentré vers midi	
Etceteré, etceteré	Etceteri, etceteri	
Ecoute-moi parler	Mais le rat est parti	
Etceteré, etceteré	Etceteri, etceteri.	

Pour voir les animaux

Je suis un grand amateur des bêtes. J'espère bien que les gens apprendront à vivre en paix avec les autres membres du royaume animal. Après tout, ils ont les mêmes droits que nous d'habiter cette planète!

I personally am a great animal lover. I hope people can learn to live together with other members of the animal kingdom. After all, they have as much right to live on this planet as we do!

Paroles & musique par/
Words & music by: Matt

Pour voir les animaux

JE SUIS ALL-É DANS LA FO-RÊT POUR FAIRE UNE PROM-E-NADE

J'AI APP-OR-TÉ MON DÉ-JEU-NER ET UN

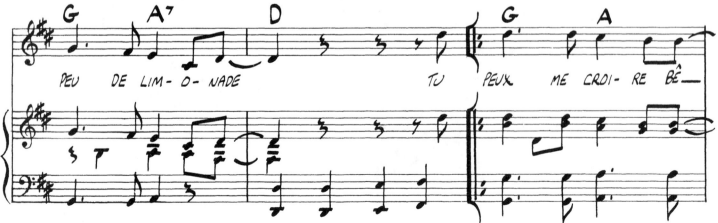

PEU DE LIM-O-NADE   TU PEUX ME CROI-RE BÊ__

J'ai vu deux grands loups
Qui couraient un peu partout
J'ai vu de beaux hibous
Qui disaient 'ou-ou-ou'

Refrain

J'ai vu un écureuil
Assis sur une feuille
Qui disait 'salut' à une sauterelle
Qui était très, très belle

Refrain

J'ai vu un grand ours blanc
Chantant une chanson
Et une douzaine de pingouins
Chantaient le refrain

Refrain

Le printemps

Ah! le printemps! Synonyme de renouveau, de fraîcheur et de jeunesse. Cela donne envie de se balader les mains dans les poches et de siffler.

Ah, spring! Everything so new and fresh and young, it just makes you want to whistle.

Le printemps

Musique/Music: Jack Grunsky
Paroles/Words: Matt

LES PET-ITS OUR-SONS SE RÉ-VEILLENT LA NEIGE EST PAR-

TIE ON EN-TEND LE BRUIT DES A-BEILLES, LE ROUGE-GORGE FAIT SON

NID. Ô LE PRIN_____ TEMPS, QUE J'AIME LE PRIN_____

TEMPS Ô LE PRIN _____ TEMPS, QUE LA VIE EST

BELLE !

Les belles fleurs dansent dans le vent
L'écureuil dit "Bonjour!"
Tout le monde semble être content
Le printemps est de retour.

Au revoir aux manteaux d'hiver
Bonjour, bottes de caoutchouc
Il y a tant de choses à faire
Quand nous jouons dans la boue.

Refrain

Nous ramassons des vers de terre
Et cherchons de belles chenilles
Et pas loin, sur l'étang
Chantent les grenouilles

Refrain (2 fois)

Comment ça va?

Paroles & musique par/
Words & music by: Matt

fine

Tout ce que je veux, c'est aimer tout le monde
Tout ce que je peux, c'est écouter
  les ondes
Oh, que j'adore chanter des chansons
Oh, que j'adore danser en rond

Comment ça va, est-ce que tu sais?

Répétez la première strophe

Comment y aller?

Paroles & musique par/
Words & music by: Matt

OÙ   VOUL-EZ-VOUS ALL-   ER   MON-

SIEUR DU-BE´?   " JE   VEUX   ALL-ER

AU   SO-LEIL"   COMM-ENT Y ALL-EZ VOUS MON-

29

EN AV- ION, EN SOU-COUPE VO.-LANTE,

EN CAM- ION COMM-ENT___ Y ALL-

ER - ER - ER EST-CE QUE VOUS SA___

VEZ _____ EST-CE QUE VOUS SAV___

Où voulez-vous aller, Madame Dubé?
"Je veux aller à Saint-Tropez"
Comment y allez-vous, Madame Dubé?
"Je vais y aller à poney"

En bateau, par le métro, en paquebot, à vélo
À pied, à poney, en train ou dans un bain,
Comment y aller, est-ce que vous savez?
Est-ce que vous savez comment y aller?

Où voulez-vous aller, Monsieur Gros?
"Je veux aller à Toronto"
Comment y allez-vous, Monsieur Gros?
"Je veux y aller en bateau"

À mobylette, à motocyclette, en tricycle,
  à bicyclette
En ballon, en avion, en soucoupe volante,
  en camion
Comment y aller, est-ce que vous savez?
Est-ce que vous savez comment y aller?

Comment y aller, est-ce que vous savez?
Est-ce que vous savez comment y aller?

Bonjour Monsieur

Paroles & musique par
Words & music by: Matt

J'ai mal aux joues
J'ai mal aux genoux
J'ai mal au cou
J'ai mal aux coudes
J'ai mal aux yeux
J'ai mal aux cheveux
J'ai mal partout

J'ai mal au dos
J'ai mal aux épaules
J'ai mal aux cils
J'ai mal aux sourcils
J'ai mal aux doigts
J'ai mal aux bras
J'ai mal partout!

Bonjour Monsieur, comment ça va?
Ça va bien?
Ô non, mon vieux
Ça va très mal.

Ma mère m'envoie-t-au marché

Une de mes chansons québécoises préférées. N'hésitez pas à ajouter vos propres paroles…même les plus folles! Au marché, vous pourriez acheter un hippopotame, un singe etc…

This is one of my favorite folk songs from Québec. If you want you can add more verses; the more outrageous, the better! At the market, you could get a hippopotamus, a monkey, etc…

Ma mère m'envoie-t- au marché

Traditionnelle/Traditional

MA MÈRE M'EN-VOIE- T'AU MAR- CHÉ

C'EST POUR DES SAB-OTS ACH- ET - ER MA MÈRE M'EN-VOIE- T'AU MAR- CHÉ

C'EST POUR DES SAB-OTS ACH- ET- ER MES SAB- OTS FONT DINE DONE DAINE

DINE DONE DAINE FONT MES SA- BOTS JE-NE SUIS PAS MAR- CHAND, MA MÈ-RE

POUR DES SAB-OTS ACH-ET-ER

D.S.

...C'est pour un canard acheter
Mon canard fait: couin, couin, couin
Mes sabots font: dine, done, daine...

...C'est pour un chaton acheter
Mon chaton fait: miaou, miaou, miaou
Mon canard fait: couin, couin, couin
Mes sabots font: dine, done, daine...

...C'est pour un tambour acheter
Mon tambour fait: boum, boum, boum...

...C'est pour un beau chien acheter
Mon beau chien fait: oua, oua, oua...

...C'est pour un poisson acheter
Mon poisson fait: glou, glou, glou...

Je ne sais pas

Qui n'a jamais posé une question restée sans réponse! Le plus important, c'est de savoir être heureux. Pouvez-vous penser à des questions qui n'ont peut-être pas de réponse?

Have you ever asked questions that your folks couldn't answer? The truth is, there are questions no one has the answer to. But as long as you know how to be happy, then you know the most important thing…Can you think of some questions that are hard to answer?

Je ne sais pas

Paroles & musique par/
Words & music by: Matt

PA - PA EST-CE QUE JE PEUX TE

PAR - LER ?

OUI , MON FILS , QU'EST-CE

QUE TU VEUX?____ DIS !   PA- PA , J'AI DES

QUES -TIONS À TE PO- SER   OUI, MON FILS,

POSE- LES VAS- Y !

POUR- QUOI ___ LE CIEL EST - IL BLEU? ____

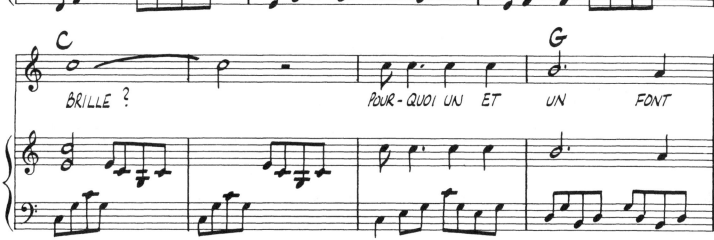

GRAND   ET   QUE JE SUIS   PE - TIT   MAIS JE

SAIS AU-SSI QUE J'AIM - E LA VIE _____

fine

Pourquoi les arbres sont-ils verts?
Pourquoi les fleurs sont-elles jolies?
Pourquoi les poissons sont-ils dans la mer?
Et qu'est-ce que c'est que la vie?

Je ne sais pas, je ne sais pas
Je ne sais pas, pose-moi une autre question
Je ne sais pas, je ne sais pas
Je ne sais pas, pose-moi une autre question

Papa, tu sais peu de choses
Oui, mon fils, c'est bien vrai
Papa, est-ce que tu peux me dire
Ce que tu sais?

Je sais que le monde est grand
Et que je suis petit
Mais je sais que je suis content
Je sais que le monde est grand
Et que je suis petit
Mais je sais aussi
Que j'aime la vie

Je suis un artiste

Cette chanson s'accompagne très bien à différents instruments de musique: violons, flûtes à bec, tambours etc…Ou bien, il n'est rien de tel que l'imagination.

This is a good song for a group of people who play different instruments: violin, recorder, drums, etc. You can also play it on imaginary instruments.

Je suis un artiste

Traditionnelle/Traditional

De la pianette!
De la pianette!

Refrain

De la guitarette!
De la guitarette!

Refrain

De la tambourette!
De la tambourette!

Refrain

Quel miracle

Il y a des miracles partout dans le monde, il n'y a qu'à bien regarder…le scintillement d'une poignée de sable, l'éclat argenté de la rosée du matin, le sourire d'un bébé…

There are miracles everywhere in the world if you have the eyes to see… Diamonds in a handful of sand, silver in the morning dew, a smile on a baby's face…

Quel miracle

Traditionnelle/Traditional
Traduction par/Translation by: Matt

QUEL MI - RACLE, ___ QUEL GRAND MI -

RACLE QUI VIT DE - DANS

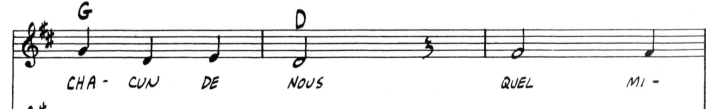

CHA - CUN DE NOUS QUEL MI -

Un sourd qui n'entend aucun bruit   *Refrain*   Les étoiles brillent, un arc-en-ciel
Ecoute une belle musique infinie   La lune, le tonnerre, le soleil éternel

English
Lyrics

Rock 'n Roll Frère Jacques

Words and music by: Matt

Are you sleeping, Brother James, Brother James?
Are you sleeping, Brother James, Brother James?
Ring the morning bell
Ding, dang, dong, dong
Ding, dang, dong. . .

Are you dancing, Brother James, Brother James?
Are you dancing, Brother James, Brother James?
We're playing, we're playing Rock 'n Roll!
Ding, dang, dong, dong
Ding, dang, dong. . .

It's Halloween

Words and music by: Matt

Ooh! The witches are coming out tonight
The ghosts are coming out too
The sky is all dark
The clouds are gray
Are you afraid of nasty spirits?
Oh, Sir, yes, yes, yes!

Refrain
It's Halloween
It's Halloween
Hey! It's Halloween
It's Halloween

At Halloween,
You can be what you want to be
A ferocious tiger
Or a blue snake
It's getting late. Are you going back home?
Oh, Ma'am, no, no, no!

Refrain

The moon is full
The owl is screeching
Bats are hanging
From every branch.
Are you afraid of this night?
Oh, Ma'am, yes, yes, yes!

Refrain

The Angora Cat

Traditional—new verses by: Matt

Once upon a time
Etc., etc.
There was an angora cat
Etc., etc.
Who was hunting rats
Etc., etc.
In the Sahara desert
Etc., etc.

He caught
Etc., etc.
In a sack of rice
Etc., etc.
A little gray rat
Etc., etc.
The size of a mouse

I'm going to eat you
Etc., etc.
"Ah yes, I know
Etc., etc.
But before having dinner
Etc., etc.
Listen to what I have to say"

"I know you're hungry
Etc., etc.
But if you really want to eat, well . . .
Etc., etc.
You should have some bread
Etc., etc.
And a little wine"

So, the cat went off
Etc., etc.
To the grocery store
Etc., etc.
He came back about noon
Etc., etc.
But the rat was gone
Etc., etc.

Woe is me, what have I done?
Etc., etc.
He got away
Etc., etc.
Now I only have
Etc., etc.
My bread to eat!
Etc., etc.

Repeat the first verse

To See the Animals

Words and music by: Matt

I went to the woods
To take a stroll
I brought my lunch
And a little lemonade

Refrain
You may think I'm foolish
You may think I'm dim
But I'll tell you
I went there
To see the animals

I saw two big wolves
Running all about
I saw two owls
Who were crying "Ooh, ooh, ooh"

Refrain

I saw a squirrel
Sitting on a leaf
Who said Hi! to a very pretty
grasshopper

Refrain

I saw a big white bear
Who was singing a song
And a dozen penguins
Sang the refrain

Refrain

58

The Springtime

Music: Jack Grusky   Words: Matt

The little bear cubs are waking up
The snow has gone away
You can hear the buzzing of bees
The robin is making its nest

Refrain
Oh, the springtime
How I love springtime
Oh, the springtime
How beautiful life is!

Lovely flowers dance in the wind
The squirrel says "Have a nice day!"
Everyone seems happy
That springtime has returned

Goodbye to winter coats
Hello to rubber boots
There are so many things to do
As we play in the mud

Refrain

We catch some worms
And look for pretty caterpillars
And not far away on the pond
The frogs are croaking away

Refrain (twice)

How Are You?

Word and music by: Matt

How are you?
Do you know?
How are you?
What are you doing?

All I know is that I don't know anything
All I know is that I feel fine
All I think is that I don't think anything
And what I feel is that I feel fine

Repeat the first verse

All I want is to love everyone
All I can do is listen to the waves
Oh, how I love to sing
And to dance about

How are you?
Do you know?

Repeat the first verse

How Will You Get There?

Word and music by: Matt

Where do you want to go, Mr. Dubé?
"I want to go to the sun"
How will you get there, Mr. Dubé?
"I'll get there by rocket"

By moped, by motorbike, by tricycle,
by bike, by balloon, by plane,
by flying saucer, by truck

How will you get there, do you know?
How will you get there?

Where do you want to go, Mrs. Dubé?
"I want to go to Saint-Tropez"
How will you get there, Mrs. Dubé?
"I'll get there by pony"

By boat, by subway, by steamship, by bike,
on foot, by pony, by train, or in a bathtub
How will you get there, do you know?
How will you get there?

Where do you want to go, Mr. Gros?
"I want to go to Toronto"
How will you get there, Mr. Gros?
"I want to get there by boat"

By moped, by motorbike, by tricycle,
by bike, by balloon, by plane,
by flying saucer, by truck
How will you get there, do you know?
How will you get there?

How will you get there, do you know?
How will you get there?

Hello, Sir

Words and music by: Matt

Hello, sir, how are you? Are you OK?
"Oh, no, my friend, things are very bad"

My nose hurts

My feet hurt

My ears hurt

My toes hurt

My forehead hurts

My chin hurts

I hurt everywhere!

Hello, sir, how are you? Are you OK?
"Oh, no, my friend, things are very bad"

My cheeks hurt

My knees hurt

My neck hurts

My elbows hurt

My eyes hurt

My hair hurts

I hurt everywhere!

My back hurts

My shoulders hurt

My eyelashes hurt

My eyebrows hurt

My fingers hurt

My arms hurt

I hurt everywhere!

Hello, sir, how are you? Are you OK?
"Oh, no, my friend, things are very bad"

My Mother Is Sending Me to Market

Traditional

My mother is sending me to market
To buy some wooden shoes
My mother is sending me to market
To buy some wooden shoes
My wooden shoes go: *dine, done, daine*
I'm not a merchant, mother,
To be able to buy wooden shoes

. . . To buy a duck
My duck goes: *couin, couin, couin*
My wooden shoes go: *dine, done, daine* . . .

. . . To buy a baby cat
My kitten goes: *miaou, miaou, miaou*
My duck goes: *couin, couin, couin*
My wooden shoes go: *dine, done, daine* . . .

. . . To buy a drum
My drum goes: *boum, boum, boum* . . .

. . . To buy a pretty dog
My pretty dog goes: *oua, oua, oua* . . .

. . . To buy a fish
My fish goes: *glou, glou, glou* . . .

I Don't Know

Words and music by: Matt

Dad, can I talk to you?
"Yes, my son, what do you want? Tell me"
Dad, I have some questions to ask you
"Yes, my son, ask them. Go ahead"

Why is the sky blue?
Why does the sun shine?
Why does $1 + 1 = 2$?
And what is life?

"I don't know. I don't know
Ask me another one
I don't know. I don't know. I
  don't know
Ask me another one"

"I know that the world is big and that I
  am small
But I know that I'm happy
I know that the world is big
And that I am small
But I also know that I love life"

Why are trees green?
Why are flowers pretty?
Why do fish live in the sea?
And what is life?

"I don't know. I don't know.
  I don't know
Ask me another one
I don't know. I don't know.
  I don't know.
Ask me another one"

Dad, you don't know very much
"Yes, my son, it's true"
Dad, can you tell me what you *do*
  know?

"I know that the world is big and that I
  am small
But I know that I am happy
I know that the world is big
And that I am small
But I also know
That I love life"

I Am an Artist

Traditional

I am an artist
Who comes from Rimouski
"We are artists
We come from Rimouski"
And I know how to play...
"And we know how to play..."
The clarinette!
"The clarinette!"

The pianette!
"The pianette!"

The guitarette!
"The guitarette!"

And the "drumette!"
"And the 'drumette'!"

What a Miracle

Traditional Translated by: Matt

What a miracle
What a great miracle
Lives inside each one of us

What a miracle
What a great miracle
Lives inside each one of us

A man blind since birth
Describes a dazzling sun
A man blind since birth
Describes a dazzling sun

A deaf man who hears no sound
Listens to limitless, beautiful music

Refrain

The stars shine, a rainbow
The moon, the thunder, the never-dying sun